# House
# of
# Muscle
# &
# Bone

M. Anne Sweet
Poetry & Art

# House of Muscle & Bone
A Studio SixEight Book

ISBN 979-8-9952168-0-3
Library of Congress Control Number: 2026906419




For contact information, visit
studiosixeight.com

Seattle, WA, USA

# POETRY BEYOND THE SPOKEN WORD

## A Rhythmic Exchange of Language and Drums

The performance group Zebra was an ongoing and evolving collaboration with more than 30 years of history. Visual artist and musician Chuck Smart (1941–2008) bridged and facilitated that rich period of creative exploration, and there were hundreds of musicians, artists, poets, and dancers involved in this generative work.

In its last configuration, we were a poet and three percussionists – M. Anne Sweet, Kate Modic, Bob Thompson, and Smart – who employed poetry, song, clapping, and world instruments in what was a literary (poetry) based art form with a contemporary approach. Our combined travels (Europe, Africa, Cuba, Indonesia) and studies allowed us to view these ideas from vastly different perspectives that challenged us to collaborate in interdisciplinary ways with an emphasis on rhythm – rhythm in language and rhythm in music.

Language puts ideas into a rhythmic system. In its written and verbal form, words are used to exchange ideas through imagery and metaphor. The percussionists, through the use of drums, shakers, flutes, and/or pan pipe, create a rhythmic system of language in order to communicate color and texture and, one might say, put the spoken word into a metaphorical context of weather and environment. They are as much poets as the poet is a rhythmist.

The poems and the poetic rhythms in this book were influenced in direct and potent ways by working with the musicians, percussionists, and dancers. It is only fitting that I dedicate this book and these poem-songs, to those fellow artists – especially to visionary Chuck Smart.

For nearly 30 years, as of 2025, I have also worked with a group of writers and artists known as The Seattle Five Plus One. Over the years the number of exceptional artists, whether literary or visual, has waxed and waned, but the core group remains steadfast. Currently, we are Jack Remick, Priscilla Long, Geri Gale, Frank Araujo, and myself. We have lost key and beloved members due to their passing – notably Jo Nelson and Irene Drennan. Many others have passed through and each has each left their own unique influence.

Throughout it all, we have supported and nurtured each other without impinging on each others' voices or styles. We have encouraged, cajoled, and challenged each other to continually raise the level of our craft, while deepening the imagery, metaphors, rhythms, and music of the language.

I dedicate this book to each of these artist-comrades as well. I thank each of them for their support and their many, many contributions to my work over all of these years. This body of work is as much a part of them as it is a part of me, and I would not be the artist I am without them. I hope I have given something of the same in return.

In particular, I thank talented and accomplished writers Priscilla Long and Geri Gale, who took time from their own creative pursuits to read this manuscript and provide valuable insights, improvements, and corrections. It is better because of them.

Deep and heartfelt thanks to the inimitable Jack Remick, deep thinker and writer, who helped me to break through the concept of "crunching images" all those many years ago. Little did we know that it was just the beginning of a long and fruitful poetic/artistic journey.

Thanks also to Paula Lowe, who encouraged me to create and include the drawings herein.

Last but not least, I thank my love and life partner, George Hopkins, for his never-ending, never-wavering support of and belief in my creative endeavors.

# CONTENTS

## RUM TEARS



House of Muscle and Bone

House
of
Muscle
&
Bone

# Enter into His Gates with Thanksgiving

Enter naked
Do not cover your growling bowels
or the incarnate ache of groinal desire
your vaginal vérité

Enter into His gates
the well where waters rise
A bamboo shaft
cups buttermilk to your lips

Womb's tectonic shift births you
in a tidal wave of moans
you wail your lost home
of muscle and bone

Orange and coconut fall
unbidden
Exit as you entered
from the waterwell
naked   breastless   untethered

# Freckle Face

Do my freckles make me
a person of colour?
Irish, Scotch, English, German
My heritage says no

But relentless taunting —
*Freckle Face, Freckleface*
*You are a freckle face* —
told me I'm different

Singing off-key
a warbler among songbirds
my spotted tint darkened in summer

Sister and I   tormented pixies
until the day the Avon lady
arrived at our door

Starstruck   we stared —
a leopardess
blue eyes, red lips, pixie-short hair
spotted  like us

# freckleface, freckleface

# Blood Web

*For Patty*

Sister –
Tell me of the black hole
that burst in your brain
a stroke of pain
tangled blood-web broken

Tell me how you held on
held to our mother's hand
held God thank-yous tight in your teeth

Tell me how you grasped
our father's hand
a milk bottle blossom
one year   a day   the setting sun

Tell me of your barefoot walk
across a blackened forest floor
how you bear the weight
Icarus burning his wings

Tell me how I pinched you
till my hands shook
a tale of Thai orchids, *krathongs*,
sins afloat in a pool

Speak Christ's love
I push you away
you of first nylons and first communion
me of first piercing   first stain

But Sister –
Tell me how a hole burst in your brain
and I listen
pray    call home
send carnation and lily
tell you   rise again
a pastor tending your sheep

You are the tower of Pisa
Noah of ark
tablets handed from a burning bush

I am the family bard

Tell me how you held on
and I will sing you rooted
a seed
          one seed
                    one sapling
                              an oak

# House of Muscle and Bone

An angry horse ridden headlong
I do not gallop these roads blinker-blinded

I have grazed with spirits
drunk from their fire stream
felt the touch of wrapt arms
I have taken their bit in my teeth
gnashing its cold steel
bridle taut on my face
reins slapping my neck

I have galloped the wide open plains
I have heart-pounded battlefields
nostril-tasted the burn
of musket and meat
I have cooled my ankles
in blood-red ponds, my head dropped

Sisyphus, I have dragged bodies
one and one and one

I have stood in meadows
under night skies
seen the stars of Tibetan steppes
I have felt the scorch of Ivory Coast
gazed at Jerusalem's walls
heard the trumpet of elk

I am the bones of my ancestors
my history written in their shins
my lungs filled with their wind

# Mother

I am what she once was
She empties her hand in mine
grips the buzzing bee
hip and knee replaced
the bone cup that birthed us  broken
this bone cradle fails her
eighty years spent in its hammock
bruises surface yellow and brown

A rat terrier snaps at my leg
tear duct waterfalls rage
razor-edged what-ifs take aim

Our mother of many mouths
rides a wheeled horse
aches for a plum breeze
We, her many
gather carrots and chrysanthemums
mend the broken water pipe
wash and fold
weed
wend aspen-gold leaves

Slow bones knit
six steps out   six back
what-ifs flutter into fall
She water-walks winter's chill

I am what she once was
fruit ripened and plucked
In spring her cane will bear
her barren limbs

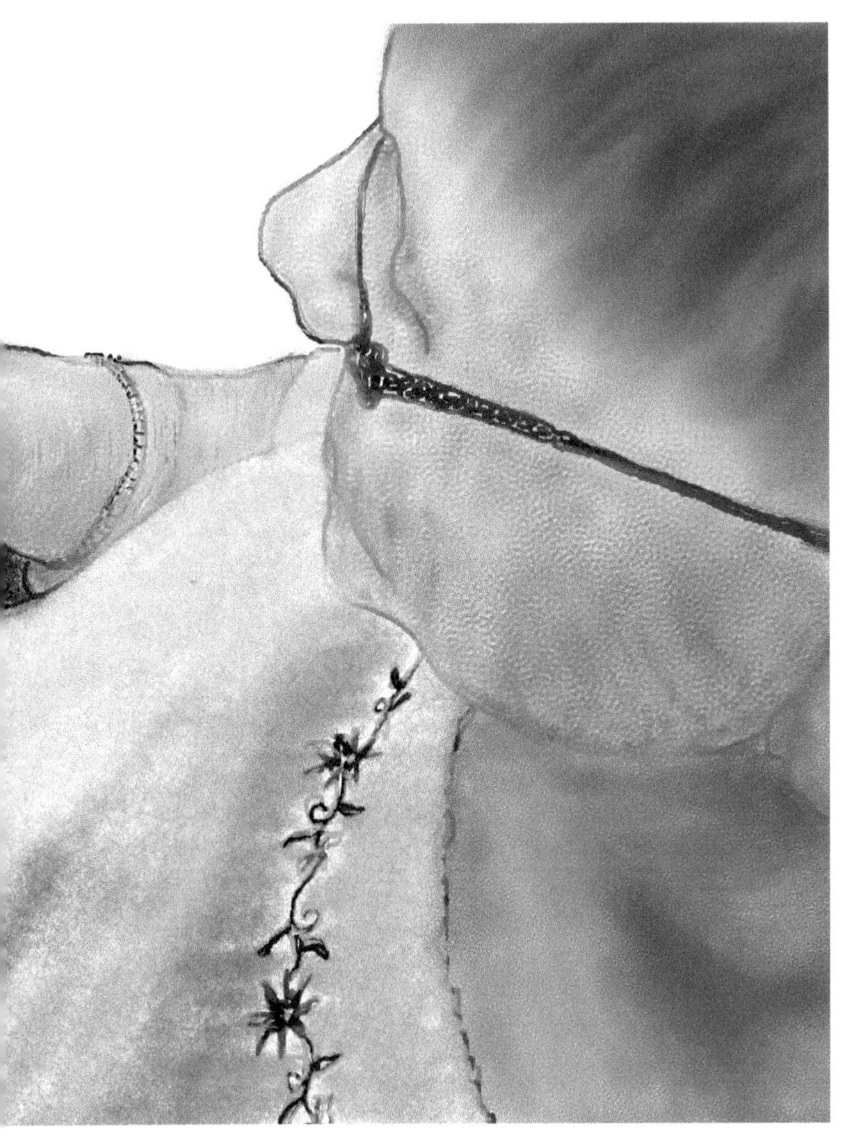

What She once was

## Cello Suite

My mother a cello
her belly full
her refrain a choral chord.
The wind is my father
his bow rubs her strings
his bellows inflate her lullabies.

She does not bend
where his hand touches her neck
where his legs wrap her curves
his knee in her side.
He presses her heart
major and minor
tremorous fingers
on the notes he bows.

His breath is the wind she yawns
His wide arm in flight is a white crane
that picks gnats from her back.
And she,
she is the wood resonance
for his vibrato.

*Mother*

# Seamstress

She stitches
quilts a river
threads
a crosshatched map

The lamb bleeds
fingers sever aorta from breath
a pink ribbon frays
sinew sticks to her hand

Stitches skew
buttons lose their grip
Her needle snags a ragged edge
heartcloth rends

She knots
sews the torn and rent
frets a seam she cannot mend

She wool-weaves the waxy wound
darns the cotton toes of socks
patches the sieve pockets of pants
She stitches the wrong all right

# Descendant

I.

I am Mirabel
Mirabel Anne
descend'd from Hannibal Hamlin
Maine senator
Abe Lincoln's first VP

On this day my mother Mirabel
her thin skin torn
bandage bled through
cannot contain the pain

We are white
I am white  feckless  freckl'd
I yearn for Hannibal
swarthy-skinn'd
abolitionist
politics sway'd against him

I do not yearn
for Andrew Johnson
Tennessee Governor
War Democrat
Lincoln's second VP
I do not yearn
for Johnson's drunken inaugural

I do not yearn
for John Wilkes Booth
at Ford's Theatre
on Good Friday night
I do not yearn
for the bullet

to the back of Abe Lincoln's head
during the funniest line of the play

I do not yearn
for President Johnson
for Confederate amnesties
Black codes
Reconstruction betray'd

I yearn for Hannibal
for what President Hamlin
might have said
    Rest assur'd
    I would be true to the great principles
    of justice and equality to all.

II.

I am Mirabel
Mirabel Anne
descend'd from my mother Mirabel
from her mother Mirabel
from her mother's mother Mirabel
nam'd for my Aunt Anne
for whom my mother Mirabel warn'd
daughter  do not say
that Hannibal was swarthy
that he may have been black
do not say
we are not pure
we are not white
we are not DAR

Mother
Lincoln left us
pure white

wast'd    water'd down
we steal what is not our own
blue-black rhythms
brought from ivory shores

Without wit
Lincoln betray'd us
left us
in Johnson's impeach'd
pure white hands
not accounting for freedmen
swarthy skin
for thin skin torn

Mother
we are descend'd
from black skin blister'd
beatings
bandages bled through
we cannot contain the pain

Mother
daughter
descend'd from Hannibal
I yearn for the hist'ry
President Hamlin might have writ

feet

# Listen to Your Mother

I am your mother
the birth-blood on your forehead
a fedora
the milk nipple
a trough gone dry
I am coyote cry
that curls from your throat
spittle that chokes your forlorn moan
the wolf's rattling howl
I am Pontius Pilate
the hammer
the nail
the washer of feet
I am Mary
the Christ cut on your side
a salt tear in your wound
I am the ivory and the ebony
keys   the fingers
of your masturbation
I am your wedding bed
I am a high heel
a mink stole
a rabid wolverine
I am a low-cut vamp
the cleavage between your toes
I am your embryonic home
a flood-ravaged slough
the slough
the flood
the valley floor
I am a crouched and rocking niño

the sliver in your bare feet
I am a hundred year old cello
the hollow of a bell
the hairs you pluck
a match head you strike with your nail
I am clavé
I am the dance
I am cobblestone
an asphalt drive
the scrape on your knee
I am the cave you spelunk
the knot in your groin
a splint
a strand of DNA
I am a cable-stayed bridge
rust   green
patina on your pewter lips
I am the wolf-whistle
you tongue in your teeth
ceramic
porcelain
the vessel of your wont
I am a tuner seeking electric vibes
a rod
a diviner
a seeker of rain
I am a vibrator
a vein on the back of your wrist
the blue vein that stiffens
underbelly's thin skin
I am frog legs
bullion
a knuckle of bone

I am basting sauce
butter, reduced onion and wine
the taste in your lover's mouth
I am the accelerator
the wheel in your hands
the gears you rev
I am the cigarette you drag
the butt you flick away
I am the crack in your blistered lip
the salve
eucalyptus
your boyish fumbling under a sheet
I am the sheet
the wing pocket from which you fly
I am the Torah
I am your mother
I am the best kiss you ever had

The black
The brown

# Lady Liberty

*"The idea, it is everything."*

> *— Victor Hugo, on seeing the
> Statue of Liberty in France
> just weeks before his death*

I.

O say can we see
the sea not shorn
and she
not free
not explicated
not shackled
but anchored patine feet
Her satin robe
stiffens against the slavish wind
her torched arm
shut down
her lighted crown
lightning grounded
Eiffel's iron armature
copper wrought
six-inch sway and 24k glow
French-gifted pieces of torch
wash again the Jersey shore
Ducks dive below
grey-green
the color of her nails

I   I   I
The song of
life

puberty
pursuit

Black Tom and Nine One One
cast us out
She the stone-cold
stone whore
our free, our masses
our immigrant tears
stained
she the black
the brown
the green patine
Madonna
suffer not
the heretic heart
the disembodied arm
the golden heart enflamed
her rote protections
dis embow
the tired, the poor, the huddled mass
the gold immaculated flame
her declarated stone
her blesserated robes
her two alone
suffragettes boat circle
the wind-weary sheer
French kissed
her lips
her you and I
her Mickey Mouse Liberty
Baldwin's bitter yoke

NO
WAR

The pulse of cells no longer flows
crown of spikes
scepter cross
her roman-numbered hex
the Queen of Swords
the land, the free
her scaffold cocoon
her Black Tom tourniquet
her nine-eleven embolism
defibbed
flat-lined
tubal ligation
her sterile-death edifice
no edit-clacking tongue
no star-struck wise
no torch emblazed
She no more births
the mother who birthed us

II.

Midwife firecrackers
tend her birth throes
her knotted gut unwinds
her broad hips
                beget blood
                        beget bone
                                beget breath
her iron heart retorched.

# We men

bleed the mid wife knife
the cut um
the fore head thorn
the beaded gourd
blade
grass
the sun hard wooed
pine
cane
the sugar spike heel

We men bleed
dead soles
scuff
drag
bite
fin  girl  nails
hide pains
wren calls
the hideous cleave age

We spit
We slit
We shall not
We
We wake
We ache
We sing   whine   drink rum   spice spiked
and blood
the penetrated sphinct
the penile hard

the priss princesstuous
the peril loss
the perpet all rhyme
the pen ink pendulum
the dastard end of love's wet mouth

We men bleed
the day's white
the smitten drool
the cries
nay, not day-d
not pine
not brave
not bear
not feral
not rash red skin
not singe
not the curséd yowl

We men bleed
the excavated sin

We men bleed
the nippled
peeling
no now no
now drown
now prick
now blood
now love let
fall scrape fall
now elbow meat
pave

meant no
meant
no stalac tight bite
no stalag
might
no

We men bleed
the army whore
the cast a way
the swan
the rapier beak
the Leda rupted twin

The green patine

## Innocents

Born
tied to
birth umbil
I
in no
sense bought
break water
pound my mother's sides
grasp thin skin on her thighs
gasp for air
suckle cut teeth
inno-
sleep in her arms

I learn again
burn of flame
pain broken bones
spare parts rust in the yard
teenage cramp
of uter-want

and envy
's heated flood
Desire escapes
panties   lace
six-packs
rippled and hip
hugs mouth
water blessings
wedding cakes
and cherry
's first crush
Blood
red ache
I  know
what my thumb invites
cocked on the lip
of navel-waist jeans
cotton
tail emblazed
No stops

Sun
moon
in no scent
sweat harmoaneeeEE
bleed the end
of mother-birth
bright black veins of crow
sail above parchment
pine
hunt owl who night-hunt shrews
free to caw caw caw
I am not your ho'

not
yet once nested
in downy heat
bare my breast
pluck feathers till my skin bleeds
right hand to god
and when he falls from dregs of ale
stand
incensed
crow of all crows
bless the virgin
corn maid
but   know
birth's blood
innocence.

Spring wet
rites   passage
grey a tone
mint   paprika
's subtle bite
I   no
wiser now
blush pink
as rooster
pointed beak
breaks aurora
's first flush
yellow shaft horiz-
on lips
not tight
no mo'

# 1st and Pine Encounter

Man on the street tells me, You look good.
Black, bearded, he carries a guitar.
There have been others
I walked on by –
a nod, a comment,
a sly glance at white skin
edged by short-cropped top.

The light does not change.
Caught on a corner
I hear myself say, Thank you,
ask, Are you from Seattle,
do you play your guitar,
have you been here long?
He mouths vague syllables –
Spokane, yes, no, not long.

Something of his guitar he sees in me.
A slim belt hugs my waist,
the sun presses hot on black jeans,
snug hipped, long, rolled
above red sandals.
A glare of rare heat
sparks his eye.

Not the first to ask for my hand –
quarters, cash or cigarettes –
You spoke to me, he says.
The light changes,
my walk hesitates.
That is all he asks.

# Artist's Model

A chalk line snaps   my leotard
black back   blue lines
crosshatch my skin   cyan
seams the back of my legs.
I am an electric blueprint.

I chalk my hands blue
count coup
war-stripe my face
my breast
indigo   azure   true blue.

I track your canvas
with cyan footprints.
A mirror breaks where I step.
You hand me a dagger of glass
mirror bleeding red lips.

You lay satsuma   still attached
to stem and leaf   in my palm
invite me to sit
around a brass nipple
orange   blood
the sting of jazz.

You sketch
the arch of my foot
candied toes
veins
taut muscle of calf.

I offer you   the truss of my arm
stem and leaf
the orange
from my cerulean palm.

# Modeling for Chuck

From behind your camera
you tell me
you are brown not black.
I am striped –
red, yellow, blue –
wrapped in kente cloth
I am shaman
I am slave
black not white
scored by ship's manifest
my cape-wrapped shoulders
scored by your sign.

You turn my head
stretch   my neck
dissolves into breast
I am soft and pink
I am brass
I am Mona Lisa in a black dress
with painted toenails
magenta hair
and yellow cheeks.
I am a black and purple sun.
A snake haloes my head.

Your shutter teases   cajoles me.
You do not ask
but I open
dressed and undressed
a slave in a cargo hold
with pink and brass breasts

flaming hair
the solstice burning inside me.

A glare of
rare heat

# Sleep Rhythms

Dip doo wah
in her head   rhythms
dah dah dip doo wah
in sleep    in her head
bip be bop
the long shadow of sleep
the long
the long shadow of
doowahdibbidy be bop
she slips her foot
into sleep
into dream
into kid leather
heels
dip dip dibbidy
ah   black straps barely bound
bind
to burgundy nails
the pink of her heels
be bop
she longs for rain
water   beneath her arch
dah dah doo wop dee dah
she strides
dreams
strides
she dreams   legs wide
she strides long
she dreams the long shadow
the long shadow of rain
doo wah

she wakes in wet
rhythms
doowahdibbidydoowapdeedah
doowahdibbidydoowapdeedah

taut muscle of calf

# Marlin Fishing

I.

There is a drought of marlin
but you have hooked my breast
with your tongue.
You troll me with your fingers,
face reflected in my neon eye.

I take your bait,
feel the bite of blood.
I turn   dive
bend through blue fire.
Sprung steel flexes my back.

Reel me
with the undertow of your arms,
your rudder lugging against me.
Hoist me   cable to deck.
Then raise your flag,
my pointed snout.
Dock to the blare of triumphant horns.

Wet your hand on my skin,
your salt with mine.
From a bed of ice
I stare far offshore.
There is a drought of marlin
but you have hooked my breast.

II.

There is a drought of marlin
and you have hooked by breast,
but I'm down with that.
I'm so far down,
I'm looking up through blue ice.
I feel the sting of blue ice.
I feel the sting of your hook in my breast
and water against my eyes,
the sting of air.
I feel your pull,
your rudder lugging against me.
I dive, running your reel
and your arms lugging against me.
I run deeper and deeper,
your hook in my breast
and your arms lugging against me.
I rise and fall, dive and rise,
my eye catches the glint of your reel.
I run – you pull and reel.
I run – you pull and reel.
I run – you pull and reel.
I run ocean deeper to ocean and I tire.
I have taken your bait.
You reel me, lugging against you –
a blue fin
flaming the fire in your arms.
You reel me ocean to boat and I tire.
I am tired.
Gaff me.
Reel me, gaff me, hoist me.
You have hooked by breast,

hoist me cable to deck.
Gaff me, hook me, hoist me.
I am sprung steel flexing
against your deck.
I am sprung steel.
I am hooked and flexing
against your deck.
My eye catches the glint of your reel,
the glint of your hook.
My eye catches your eye.
Your face reflects in my neon eye.
There is fire in your arms.
There is flame in my eyes.
Your eye catches my eye
and there is flame.
I have taken your bait
and the flame in my eye expires.
I am fish.
I am fresh.
I am fresh fish on a bed of ice.
The flame in my eye expires.

*Mona Lisa in a*

black dress

# Penthesileia

*(Pen thu sil EE a)*

*Amazon queen known for her great
beauty and her prowess in battle;
killed by Achilles who, upon removing
her helmet, fell in love with her*


I.

Daughter of War
her armored breast
her queenlike head
her golden belt adorns
She wields her sword
her spear
her crescent shield
Sundogs hang from her ears

On her back a quiver
cedar shafts
a sinewed bow
She hunts for dove and deer
her wrists twist
her arrow errs
her sister queen is slain

She bites her lip
she bares her breast
she lactates tears
her unshut eyes
her brown-gold-pink
mountain-edged
the empty steppe
blood has shed

her sister dead
She mounts her horse
her tears have spread
she rides Aegean shores

She wages war
Achilles' dread
their shield to shield
their spear to spear
their head to head
He wants her dead

She does not dread his murder plot
she will not seek his heel
his sandaled foot
She will find his knot
his heart
his softest spot

And then she's dead

He mourns the leaded spear
that led to here
his where   his why
his she must die
he rants
he wails
his spear and sword
the shield he wields
his ward of swords
his army built
but she is dead
the world now torn
he loved her more

She downs her head
her beauty bled
she's dead
she's dead

Her life now gone
the death knell bell
the gong
the wailer's song
her life now sprung
she's gone
she's gone

A wooden boat will take her home
her bones alone
her muscle gone
her beauty stung
her wisdom won
her breast
her heart laid bare
her life now sung in word and song

The flame in her eye

II.

Between her legs
a Harley roars
her chrome
her calves
her ankles gleam
stiletto valves

her patent black
her leather thighs
her hips
her canyon deep
her belly moon
her lion heart
She will not die
her life alone

She rights all wrongs
with pen and speed
her battle song
She rides her roaring steed
with tattoo sleeve
her corset vest
her helmet head
her bling
her angel wings

Her belly band
conceals her carry
she wields

her blade
her chain
her Smith and Wesson
Her life unslain
her sister's too
she does not rue
the blood not shed
She writes all wrongs
her life now spun in word and song

Her
life
now
spun

# Chili Pepper Rap

Word is you're carryin' a Glock 9
you been holdin' for some time.
Word is you're lookin' to ice the dude
who jacked your ride
runnin' at high speed
an' butter-stained your fine seats.
Word is you're lookin' for the dude
who violated your beats.

Word is you're carryin' a Glock.

Well, Luce and me got hot
thinkin' about them red hot pepper shots.
She firecrackers her red lips
swingin' her hips
says, we got to go for a drive
send Lil over to keep Benny's ass occupied
got to borrow his wheels for the night.

Word is you're carryin' a Glock.

We drove fast and sweet
diggin' your ear-splittin' beats
so she could ace some naughty treats
long an' hot
burnin' her lips
an' butter-stainin' your seats.
I tell ya, it was hard to drive
an' I left my own butter on your hides.

Word is you're carryin' a Glock.

Lincolns spent
the cells dead
we stop at an all-night dig
Luce cooin' her give-it-to-me gig
butterin' a naugahyde stool
and I danglin' a patent black mule.
The punk fell hard for Luce and me
so eats and the phone came free.

Word is you're carryin' a Glock.

So we tried to call
but when you didn't pick up your cell
we knew Lil had your ass chilled.
an' we were cruisin'
hip hoppin' the highway
playin' with red hots
thinkin' we're his bitches
ain't no low-life snitches.

Word is you're carryin' a Glock.

Word is you're out to ice the dude.
It weren't no rude dude
it was Luce and me.
Word is you're carryin' a Glock
but you can pack that piece
all we did was leave
a little butter on your seats.

# Red Widow

I hid
I hid
I hid
black, ugly
spiderchild I wove
an alphabet
calculus cove
bound in spinneret's thread

Caved
cowered
I stare at cracks
cut by my shattered nails

A finger pokes at my chest
pecks a litany of to-dos
no crying corner comfort
just the clack of heels to floor
copier to computer
to click-worn keyboard

A widow crawls from her corner
flaunts her hourglass
taunts
    *Trust me*
    *stroke your palette*
    *knife obliterate*
    *graffiti nail-scratched*

Her belly taut
her hour running out

epigyne sterile
of egg
of sperm
she snags my hand
bites my palm
spits
    Crawl out
    seek your palpus
    wield pen and knife
    sharpen your nails
    wax your wetted brow

I crawl from my cave
Domina matrix
in whip-crack heels
poison thighed
and red lipped

# Code Talkers

Prince and pauper, you and I talk
the riddles of forgotten myth.

We talk bluebells nodding their heads
at a bed of pink chrysanthemums.
Commas fall in the phrases of fronds.

A rock tongue of granite exposes
its gnarled breast from a gravel bed
dung of seagulls strewn among crab shells.

The sorcerer unbends
his hand, exposes a cat's eye
marble the size of robin's cyan egg
a sunset prayer at water's edge
in skips of a flat rock.

Our tongues tied between us
a saliva warm rush of syllables
the G-spot erection
when my heart speaks your name.

A crow electrocutes and falls
at my feet, black sacrament.
I read between the lines –
he is the spirit of your ancestors
my ancestral cord
a cradle
a glove of grass.

# Songcatcher

She whistles on wicker legs,
winged archaic wishbones,
her naked gold eye,
a raptor with song in her teeth.
She lights in your mind,
a cave pictographed
with rust horses, boar and wild ox.
She feasts the meat of hollows,
soars the downbeat
improv of stalactites.
Drip!
The prick of moisture!

She hunts —
nails click when they land.
You offer her   calf
skin   offer to wrap her in your fore
skin   She offers you
the hide off her feet,
the dangerous red slit
where her seams part.

*Full of*

She sings two
notes   You sing three
notes   She sings papyrus
between her legs
notations   keeping score
of flute and drum,
the flit of gnat and note
dense   ass blue,
breath
the weight of a sigh.

In her claws   your kid
skin   Havana red
streaks   on albino
skin   where her nails
drip your blood,
her score regurged in your hands.

*the sound of congas*

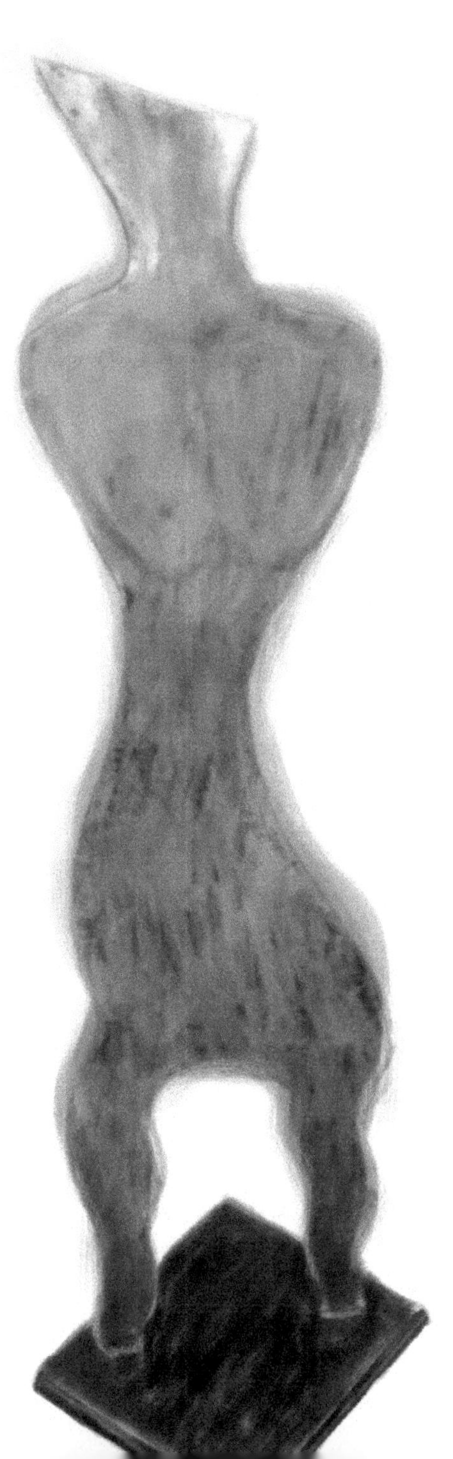

# Chuck Plays Divine

Steel –
she is steel and weld –
she is steel and weld and black swirls –
she swirls black –
she is breasts and butt –
she is stations –
stations of a drum, she is rhythm –
she is hollow –
he pats her rump –
she is sound –
she is hollow and rhythm
and full of sound –
she is full of the pat and thump
of his hand –
his thumb thumps her ribs
and she opens –
she is open and hollow
and full of the sound of congas –
he spins her on squat legs –
he spins and pats –
he slides his hand down the long slide
of her back –
she is sand –
she is sand on a beach under a hot sun
and he is the ocean –
he is a spray of sweat on her cheek –
she and he –
they are shoulder to shoulder –
breast to breast –
they are the acoustics of light and dark –
drum and voice –

they are song —
they are a mambo —
he lifts her —
she is cold and steel —
his hand is the hot beat of a samba —
she warms to his hot hand
and she opens —
she opens her throat and she sings —
she sings in drum beats —
a conga
she sings the thump and beat of his hand —
she sings his touch —
he touches her steel soul —
he touches her breasts —
her belly —
the long slide of her back —
he caresses her butt
and he lifts her —
she hot and silver —
she is swirls of black —
she is Divine —
she is in his hands
and in his hands
she is flesh
and her hollows pump with blood.

## Dis
##### dat

Deogi cat
yowls she
crawls from her cave she
a beasty in cat heat
Scarab-tipped she
                              claws he
tattoos her print she
ruby throat'd
                    butternut
He cat
          she cat
nectars
              his needle beak
sips he
              from lips she
vines he
              leg around leg she
no end or begin
Wet she
              rain he
tawnies her forest he
She rolls
              in leaf heat
hides her own
                    butterheat
He purr
              she sure
coy with her toy she
He dance
              she prance

trots past
            with swing hips
rubs he with scent lips
He roar
            she allure
flips up her tail more
She flicks
            her scarab tips
White orchids erupt
Storm hips
            seek heat
She strikes
            AIYEE! he
Cohiba
        in cave teeth
Sores on his lips he
tosses her head she
the Nile on her neck
Shango
        he tangos
burns in her mango
dis
    dat
thin
        spittle of
                Ting!

# Whisperers

For Joe Pirone and George Hopkins

I.

In my dream a man leans in
his genitals press against me
he sprays my mouth
and my arms numb
He takes me to a clinic couch
teaches me the Zen of paralysis
Bound
powerless
I wait

My arms loosen
again
the man sprays my mouth
my arms go numb
He tells me he will teach me
the Zen of sexual assault
his genitals press against me
I struggle awake
under the weight of restraint

Horse Whisperer
I feel you shank my halter
from beyond the grave
I gaze in the mirror
I hear you warn
*You are about to get fucked*
  *again*

II.

Whale whisperer
circles his hand above the water
humpbacks
he beckons their turquoise flukes
with his wave
they hear his silent call

The captain speaks
*Someone onboard has drawn them*
Whale whisperer
they spy-hop white knobby chins
rise to meet his eye
their black eyes do not break
above the cellophane sea

They follow our drift
circle yin yang below our boat
douse us with blessings of whale-rain

III.

Moons ago, Horse Whisperer
you led me
to this man I now call my own —
He and I
we met
we parted
I did not take his number
You said
*You'll have to go back*

Moons later
this man whispers to whales
and you whisper to me from beyond

Whisperer
you have led horses to grass
bade them to eat
Now your thick hands
lead me to water
I drink




*She sings in drum*

I WON'T FALL VICTIM

# The Economy of Love

*For Muqaddas Tawfeeq, 22, murdered
by her mother and brother after she
married against her family's wishes,
June 2016*

I.

Her dam spills
the gash
the bloodied bones
the child that ripens in her womb
her brother wields
the rod   the stick
the tapered knife
cuts deep her family soil
tender bodies torn

II.

Her mother's waters broke with her
her child
ripened in her wound
alluvial soils erode

III.

Waters flow downstream
deposit a delta of debris
death wounds
broken bones
a fire of flesh
to whom do we belong?

IV.

We live the stark economy of love
we live the price of meat
we live the doe
the fawn
the blood-let cries
of bellies pierced
we live the bulleted buck

We live the scarcity of love
we live the wounded womb
we live the women stoned
we live their broken bones

# Cotton Field

Midnight
white sheet
the white of an eye
scent of musk
his yoke shoulders her clavicle
an oxbow knuckles her ribs
Thou shalt not
No one to erase the chalk
scratched on her board
pluck the splinters from her ass
the stuck pig bleeds
her sailcloth sodden
Thou shalt not
weights her escape
His chicken beheaded
she covers one eye with her hand
Thou shalt not
Thou shalt not
Thou shalt not covet
mama says
cornbread ain't white
corn bread and grits
pop amber seeds
hot oil on her skin
plaid
Thou shalt nots
cover her head
Thou shalt not covet
yesterday's chitlins
birth at her knees
half & half spills

at the end of her cord
chard's red streak
collards and ham hocks
her heart is a vat
Thou shalt not covet
Thy brother's hare
midnight
under a white sheet
the white of an eye
Thou shalt not
Thou shalt not

*She holds back*

# Song of Chabaroka

*A poem for two voices and drum*

You know the journey.
I walked the sand
from Amsterdam to Afghanistan
from Nairobi to South Africa.
My name is Chabaroka.
My robes collected dust
and dung of desert toads.
My beard and hair smelled of hashish.
I knelt.
I prayed.
I heard the music.
I followed a herd of zebras.
Their black and white was a river
I crossed.

    *What about the people?*

They are black, they are white.
They are not grey.
You are white, I am black.
We are not grey.
You heard my songs
and a black panther leapt from you.

Sister,

    *What about the peoples*
    *of the world?*

I am a man as black as Africa.

I am black.
Not white.
Not grey.

    *What about the peoples?*

You are Euro-white
bleached of black
bleached of Eve.
She was your brown mother
but you have faded
brown-black stripes faded to white.

    *The black leopard's spots*
    *reflect in sun.*

I am her brown-black son.
I am black
as black as my father,
as his father,
as his father's father's father.

    *What about the mothers?*
    *What about the mothers*
    *of the world?*

On the savannah
the wind blows through grass.
There is sand.
There is a water hole
surrounded by mud.
I am my father's son.
I walk to the water.

I wait for the elephant to wallow.
I cake myself with mud.

    The lion will not smell him sweat.
    He will hunt among them.
    The zebra will not smell him sweat.
    He will urinate
    and the white master will turn away.

In my hand is a spear.
The blood will spill
the black and the white
the blood not grey,
            not black,
                not white.
The blood will spill.

    The Asian mother nurses her son.
    Her brown passes her teat.
    He swallows.
    He carries a spear.
    He is caked in mud.
    It is his birth day
    The lion does not smell him sweat.

The white mother fears
the mud-caked spear.
She holds her breath
when her babe is born.
She holds back her black, her brown.
But you were her first
and she let you slip out.

You tasted her black
and you ran.

    *I am running.*

You are running.

    *See me run.*

I ran the savannah.
I ran the grass.
I ran the black and the white.
Zebras run.

    *Who ARE you running?*

My name is Chabaroka.
I give you my name, Chabaroka,
sing my song.

    *I am singing.*

SING MY SONG.

    *I am singing.*
    *I am the white stripes,*
    *I am singing*
    *Euro-burnt in the sun.*

I feel the leopard's claws in my haunches.

    *I am singing.*
    *I am the black and the white.*

I taste the blood.
I am singing.

I am the meat the leopard feeds on
the meat he feeds to his young.
I am the blood the leopard feeds on.
The blood in his blood
the blood in his young.
My name is Chabaroka.

I am singing.

Sing my song.

I am crying.

I am the black.

I am the white.

We are the black and the white.

We are the white and the black.

The white stripes on her side.

The black spots on his hide.

I am the black
that slipped from my mother's teat.

I am the white
that slipped from my mother's teat.

What about the zebra?

    *What about the leopard?*

What about the white master?

    *What about the blood on your haunches?*

I am running.

    *I am crying.*

What about the people?

    *We are the people.*

What about the black and the white?

    *We are the black and the white.*

I knelt.
I prayed.
I followed a herd of zebras.

    *See them run.*
    *The black and the white.*
    *The white and the black.*

My name is Chabaroka.
Sing my song.

    *We are the black.*
    *We are the white.*

We are singing.

We are the peoples of the world.

What

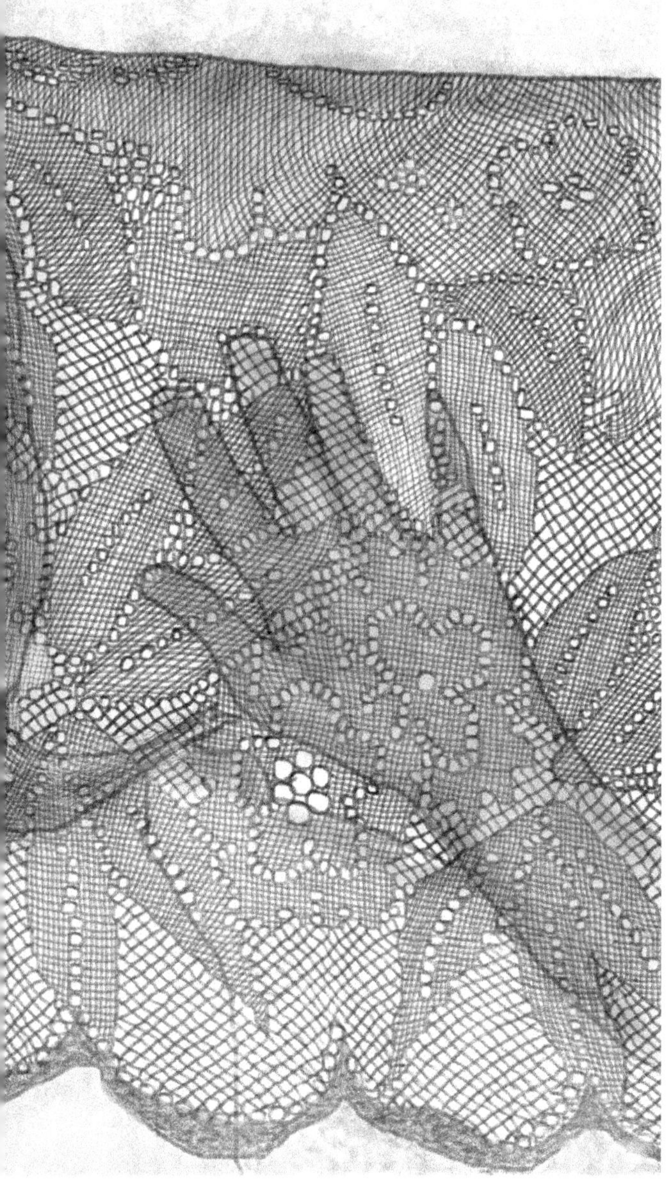

about the zebra?

### Tierra Distante

*For Carolina in Cuba*

*Un beso, mi amiga*
a kiss
a hug electron
*¡Qué bueno!*
*mi hermana español*

*Norte*
*sur*
*tierra distante*
I cannot walk
*ni tú*
our soles do not touch
*¡Qué triste!*
*¡Qué lastima!*

*Ingles y español*
we suckle
bloom
birth seeds
wither
How strange!
How strange!
*¿Qué quiere decir?*

*Tú*
*espíritu abundante*
ask the roots
ask the berries
*¡Por favor,*
*mi hermana español!*

Nosotros estamos uno
one
tierra distante
from this far soil
my small voice
lo siento,
mi corazón
my heart desires more
¡Qué la vaya bien!

about the leopard?

# Fidel Resigns

*Cuba, February 19, 2008*

Fidel
your voice over the square
commands
government offices closed
*supermercado* closed
hotels and restaurants
*los paladars*
*las casas particular*
studios, dance classes
markets and home-front
vendors of cloth dolls
and 1950 Chev model cars
gas stations, banks
the neighborhood clinic
all closed
all *madres y ninos*
all husbands and suitors
all picked up and bussed
to stand hours
under the sun
your voice
in the square
at the concrete feet of Martí

Salt sea air
polluted fog
pick at stucco and stone
Fidel
after 50 years
you do not resign.

Your body resigns
in Cuba
where nothing resigns
ancient mechanical soldiers
gnash machete teeth
lawnmowers
stressed Soviet steel
roar across neighborhoods
where nothing resigns
contraband computers
and cell phones
hidden
where nothing resigns

Thin horses
clop carriages down rutted roads
bend their heads
to days-old muffins and bread
Artists press their own papers
palette colors they can afford
Women, ruffled orishas
Obatalá, Ochún
dance on cobblestone
pose photos for coins
saints hidden
Our Lady of Mercy

What about the blood

Our Lady of Caridad
bless us
in Cuba
where nothing resigns

This day Omar tells us
they will celebrate in silence
hope for personal revolution
Marisol speaks
more English than in 10 days passed
    You are here on an historic day

Fidel
after 50 years
you do not resign
your body resigns
a revolutionary sun
at the toes of José Martí
the shadow of Che's starred cap

on your haunches?

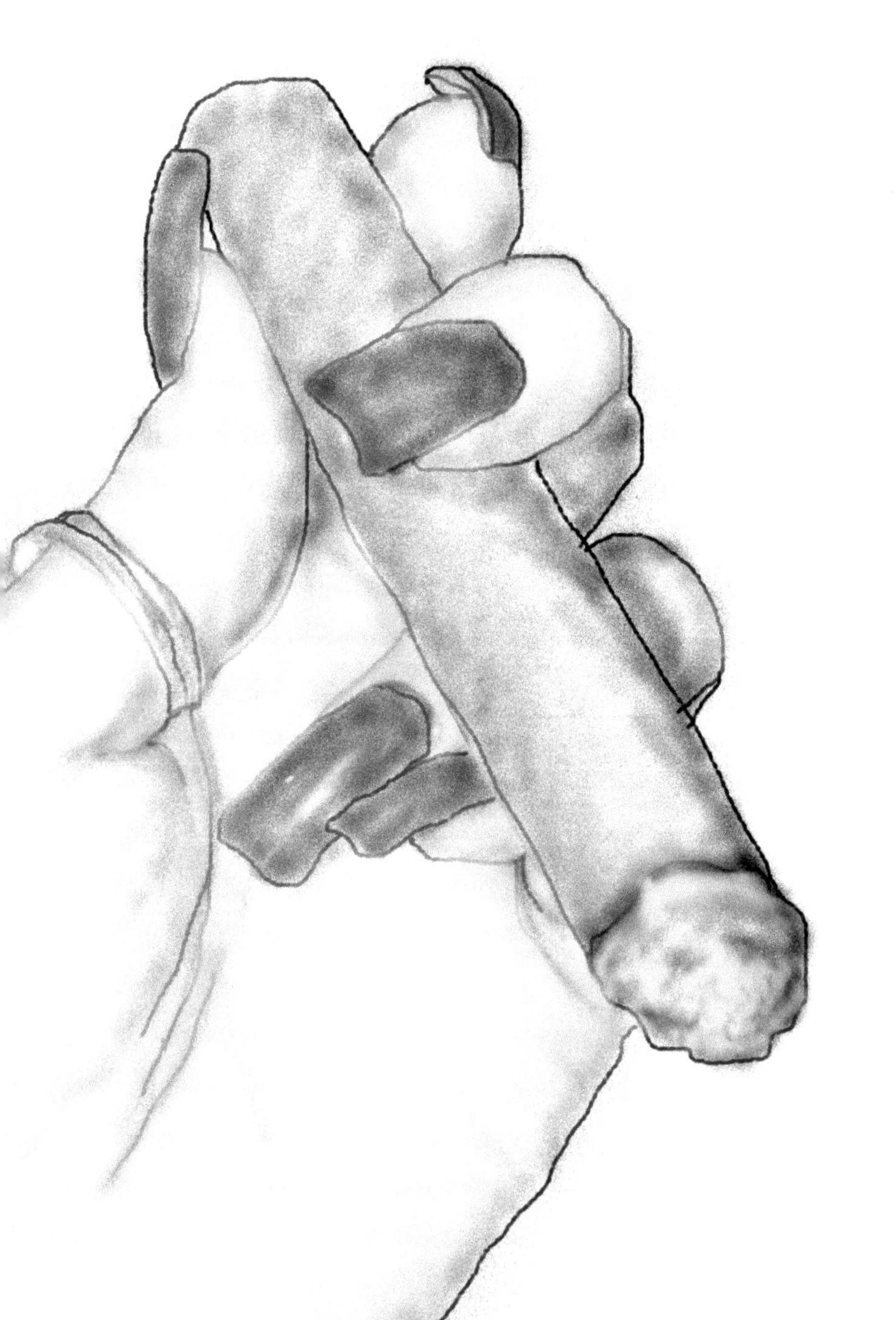

# Canto a los Orishas #1

*For Charles Morgan Smart*

Purple sunset drives its wedge
across my skull anterior,
I, cross-eyed with pain
from its bilingual shaft.
On one side is writ a prayer,
Sanskrit text weeping
the death of slaves.
On the other – Mother of God? –
the same tale told
in the tongue of Yoruba.
And here, sharp incisors have bitten
punctuation into the splintered wedge.

Behind my eyeballs, clave throbs.
Beyond the sunset   black
overcomes the purple benediction.
An apparition raises its voice,
*What lies beyond my death throes?*
*And what of north winds*
*blown from my mouth?*
*Or the westerly Chinook*
*that warmed my brothers' bones?*

Great aunt in her rocker,
cross-armed,
hums gospel hymns.
Child-chants learned
on Sunday afternoons
spill from elder lips.
I turn the last page,

sing one final verse.
A quarter note weeps a tear.
My body, soul's slave, wilts,
a minor key teething,
    I am lost,
    my youth, a diminished chord;
    a big band salsas
    and I can no longer dance.

Obatalá! Eleggua! Oggún!
I offer incense, cigars,
spit rum to the four corners.
I am a man,
a purple shaft of pain,
scholar of art and sound.

Ochún,
yellow my lips
with your honey,
the bite of rum.
Spit me,
sing me,
candle my altar.
Drink me
my mother's honey.

What about the

## Canto a los Orishas #2

Olodumare,
my back carries a cargo
of slaves splintered with hull wood,
peopled waters weighted with stone.
Behind the robes of saints
wind-scar lashes their skin.

Yemayá,
press next to me,
your blue robes, a sea of love letters
written in blood dye.
Your broad hand is an island.
Sand beads and river snails,
cowrie shells bracelet your waist.

Oduduwa,
your son divines me.
He is a yellow rod of lightning,
his copper sparks my eye.
On rainslick-tile steps,
he catches my fall,
the bloom of bruise.

Babalú-ayé
chases me down a cobblestone street,
Ochún in his hips,
rhythm of rumba on brick.

He flags down my bicycle cab,
swats flies,
pleads my address.
His voice bleeds for escape.

Oyá,
windmaid riding the tail of a horse,
gust the wings of my skirt,
clothe my bare limbs in a breeze
of coconut shell, palm frond,
banana leaf.

Our Lady of Caridad,
bend your head,
look beneath your yellow hem.
I offer a rose-colored almond,
Cohiba's paper ring,
a charm of wood beads.

Ask the roots
Ask the berries

# Notes on the Margin
### For Ernesto "Che" Guevara de la Serna

Mountain night
a man
viz only
by four white teeth
fled
the dogmatying knife
wrested
bones
seized the thing
he had become
contra   the un
adapted
sin

Asthma
fires lungs
cross hairs
purse lips
spit fruit
winnow peach bowels

Weep not
the power we
Weep not
the crumbling
will to die
the ins-true-meant
weep not
the'r evolution

*Stand*

Fist
jaw
his rogue incisor
the beehive-we
murmurs
the night-edged
howl
assaulted trench
the enemy fallen throat

Hat and nap
trans-mi-
grate
Argentine dunes
Marx
runes uncode
code
squared forth
bleat   curse
the dagger teat

Nostrils taste
the gun
stained
slain
blood
his body
*mea culpa*
*mea culpa*

Hours under the sun

# Wrong Place Story

*"It's just like putting lemon on fish."*
*– Miles Davis*


I.

18 hours and half the globe
Seattle
Taipei
Bali

Madé drives through Denpasar
wouldn't hurt a fly
but kills a fly on the steering wheel
asked why, tells us,
    *The fly – he was in the wrong place*

Buddhas and stone cats
line by line by
two-lane street
Motorcycles
two by three by
right-hand SUV
stops   blocks
He is in the wrong place

In the market
rinds and peels heap in the square
sarongs
T-shirts
vendors with arm-blocks
    *come look, come look*
hocks the air

92

Ikat hangs umber on gold
stacked navy, maroon, burnt red
tailor-made jacket, pants, buttons
what buttons, what lining, which print?
We are in the wrong place

Late night
unlit by electric moons
waiter says
    sorry
    no bagels
    no tomatoes
    no ice
wrong place

Money-changers say
    closed
    impossible
    take only American Express
The Bali dog limps
ant disappears in frog-tongue
wrong place

A Belgian in Ubud
Syrian-born
Oussaid unpacks
pouch after pouch
antique gold sun rises
$480 just-to-try bracelet
latch jams on my wrist
wrong place

Medicine bottles
fall where they stand
Holy coral snakes
curl in a cave
Monkey hand
grabs hat, bag, pocket
sniffs hair
looks for monkey reflected
in camera lens
wrong place

Temple 1,000 steps down
Dawn blessed by machete blood
1,000 steps up
90-degree heat
80 percent sweat
Exit visa lost
behind dragon pants
wrong place?

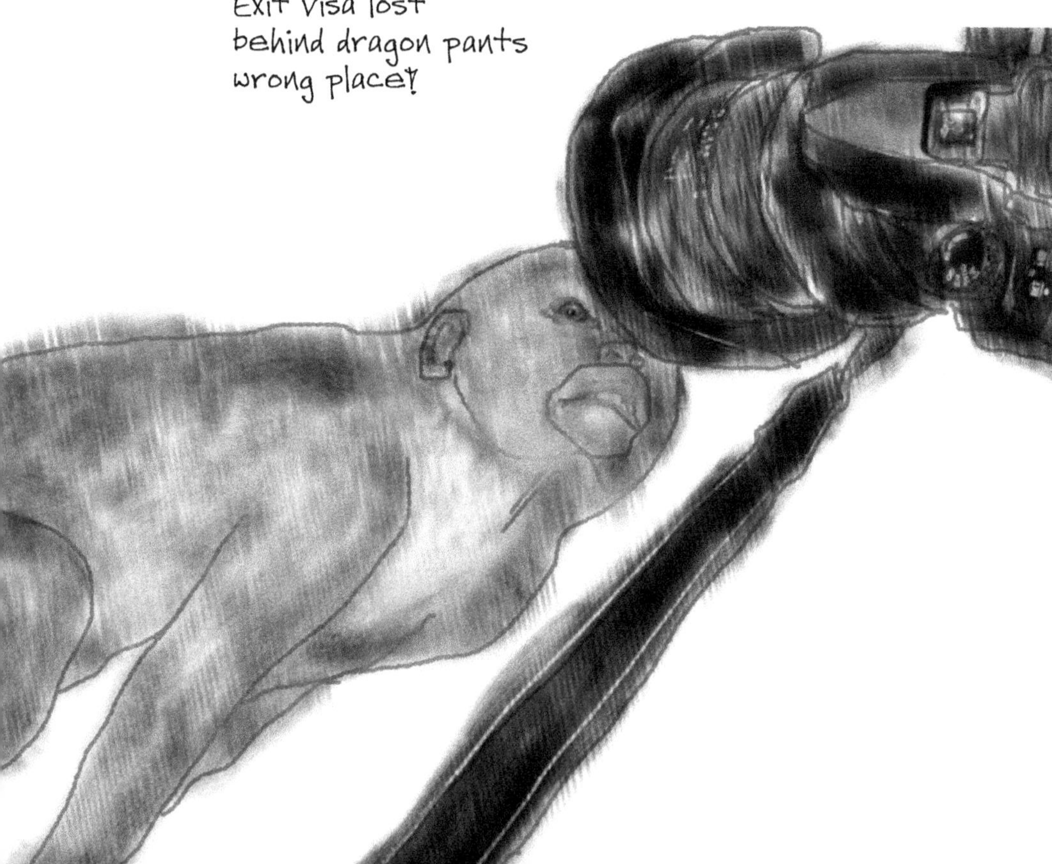

II.

Seattle
Taipei
Ubud

Our two-week home
marble
tile
teak and mahogany
open-air kitchen
and offerings
beside the pool
papaya, mango
melon and jackfruit

20-foot monkey gods
stucco and thatch
rice paddies
frog-song
    *Selamat pagi,*
     *apa kabar?*
     *Baik, baik, kam u?*
We are in the right place

Dewa offers water
shade of The Lotus
carp reflect in glass pool
umber, maroon, burnt red
Nyoman Naia ties Chinese knot buttons
fits my black slacks
A peacock unfurls on my back
right place

Red flags
unfurl black bulls
a stage of red shirts
Megawati – they want her to win
offer drinks
young man strips off his red shirt
says
   *For me*
means
   *For you*
    *Here – a flag for your car*
right place

Agung Rai
Museum of Art
a wedding
of gamelan and gongs
mallets and brass scales
Kecak under the full moon
   *chak, chak, chak*
men checkered
black and white
serpentine back to breast
   *chak, chak, chak*
brown arms
branch and sway

Egrets fly north by north
by dusk
heron the village
palm by palm by flock
eels swim to the hook
bamboo penjors bend overhead

dangle palm leaf gold sun rises
a bracelet of rice paddy song
gecko and *kodok, kodok*
call and respond
we are in the right place
    *Baik, baik*
    *Terima kasih*
right place

Light a cigar

# The Writer's Words
### After "The Artist's Smoke" and "Patrice: A Poemella," by Geri Gale

Confession 1

I am a writer who rarely reads.
It is not my wont.
I have forgotten
the intimate isolation
absorbing alchemy
biography or fiction –
the precipice of life lived.
Poetic truffles are my sustenance
succulent, short-lived
they melt thin on my tongue.
I long for vegetable matter and meat.

Ear Buds 1

The ritual begins –
a plane
a buckling
a seat on the aisle
wait –
for the engines, the taxi
the backward pull of Gs against my chest
lift off
the litany of emergency
finally
the okay for electronic device.

From under the seat
book, iPad
ear buds uncurled
click to shuffle
Miles and Thelonius
volume envelopes
pages open
I am alone with the writer's words.

<u>Flight 1</u>

Outside the air stretches
Washington Oregon Wyoming
across a corner of Colorado.
Inside the cabin thin air
words pressure-fill my lungs.
I am locked in
a word junkie voyeur
until
I feel our descent
forced to land
forced to decompress
disembark
forced to close the book.

<u>Ferry 1</u>

Now  without the solitude of flight
I seek a solitary ritual
float by ferry

starboard soliloquy
a sounding
I cross and recross
isolated by ear buds
immersed in a merciful sea.

<u>Home 1</u>

In the bathroom
behind closed doors
I plead to be left alone
tie off my left arm
tap the vein –
the writer my lover
feeds me sweet meats
cream sauce
a heroine that leaves me floorbound
foolish
forgetful to feed the cats.

<u>Smoke 1</u>

Cocooned
she gives me a room with a view
a bridge and a red velvet couch.
She gives me a match to strike
the rich, earthen smell of tobacco lit.
She gives me a century to live and to die.
I read
inhaling the artist's smoke.

# Fire and Stone

Priscilla Long's *Fire and Stone*
consumed me –
art and science mixed with memoir
memoir mixed with science and art
wit and humor   sadness and loss
passion and life lived
I entered –

Abecedarian.
Ancestors. Adam. Amen.
Ablutions.
Acts that see to the maintenance of life.
A world replete.
Books. Brains. Blindsight.
Beautiful, bullet-proof dress.
Bowls of stones. Bucket.
Boogie-woogie. By yourself.
Cave of calm concentration.
Companion of the crossover.
Clawhammer banjo. Clone.
Darwin's long shadow.
Dread of sudden disappearance.
Disgusted domesticity
   disgorging its dis-contents.
Dairy cows.
Einstein. Eve.
Erudite, amateur botanist.
*Esse Quam Videri.*
Emotional stones.
Fox head, fox tail, fox ears, fox paws,
   small fox face.

Fear grimace.
Funerary figures. Fire.
Grandmother ape. Ghost swans.
Greenbrier. Global warming.
Home-funneled sun fueling the grid.
Homo sapiens.
Hippocampal activity. Hands thick with work.
Homo sapiens sapiens.
Hominin.
Ham and Enos.
Headstrong humorous harangue.
Inheritance. Inheritor. I am home.
Identical twin.
Ink made of inkberries.
Invasive species.
Johnsontown. Jalopy.
Jazz is the key to Mondrian.
Keening of crows. Kennewick Man.
Killer headaches.
Loss of ecosystems.
Love and death and sorrow and dinner.
*Liberté, Egalité, Fraternité*
Monarch butterflies. Milkweed.
Muse in the church of poetry.
Moody monologue.
Moravian Seminary for Girls.
Neandertal.
No one else can play the music
   you are given to play.
Neil singing the blues.
One of the Great Minds of the West.
Over-rehearsed rhinoceros.
Oh! Look! We can read!

O Say, Can You See. Past is prologue.
Pammy and Poky. Paradise.
Pegasus. Peacock coal.
Paid homage in droves and swarms and flocks.
Poems are my prayers.
Quietude.
Quest for quiet.
Quaker Neck Road.
Rapists.
Receptive to Guan Yin.
Rigid, religious, rule-ridden.
Required to play the psaltery.
Sock Mountain. Still as stone.
Silence and slanted sunlight.
Sunlight buried.
Susanne.
Time enough and space enough.
Theosophy.
Ur-cells. Universal truths.
Very funny, Mother.
Vessels from which my genes were poured.
Writing. Walter Long. Winslow.
We wonder. We Three Big Kids.
Xenial xeroxes.
Yellow piping on puff sleeves.
Yoga. Zeppy.
Zen.

*The ritual begins*

Rum
Tears

**For**

*For those killed
in the World Trade Center,
September 11, 2001;
for Sasa and for Julio*

You    me
dog got your back    me
I light a cigar

                   and smoke

you and she
bow
at the Buddha head
with incense
yellow flowers

                   and smoke

Sasa

        barks    wags
at your back
no more

              Julio
at your back

                  no more

drums
brother and spirit
she    he

                crushed

by their own
bodies

           many
under towers
brick

        smoke

girders broken
and backs
St. Helen's
                dust

Me   you    she
together
            apart
                    we
grieve
for other
            the others
you   she
at the Buddha
incense
        rum tears
                stone




and slanted sunlight

# Sign Language
### For Jo Nelson

Leaf bones laid across my shoe
by the wind   her hand   no small mistake.
She drops leaves
Dylan Thomas at my feet
tells me
Lorca is the ghost who follows her.

She speaks in bones
left on a hill   beside the well.
I climb her mountain.
Holly and maple wail at my feet.
She speaks in leaves.
Listen – a single leaf falls
where no tree stands near.

She speaks in a rose gown
at night   beside my bed
aspen leaves caught in her hair.
She speaks at dawn
caped   red over Olympic peaks
her smile beaked
goose feathers fly from loose braids
as she dances   raven on sandaled feet.

She speaks in signs
left beside the road.
A heron lands in the ditch.
An eagle hunts low on the beach.
I follow – for three miles her wingtip
fingers my hair.

# To Irene
## on the Anniversary of Her Death
*For Irene Drennan*

We drink her funeral beer
blood wine
stingers of bees
her pierced body broken

Dying, she leaves us her wounds
her flesh raw
her savory   her sweet
her apple allegories
sashimi
pastries
the tree-grown orange
vinegar's bitter bite

# Mary's Song

*For Mary T. "Songless Dancer" McQuillen*
*(1932–2007)*
*March 21, 2007, Spring Equinox*

Pneumonia
her death takes
Makah memories
and oral historicals
high-born tribal elder
born on March 9 1932
to Florence and Walter
in Neah Bay
her life
wisdom brought to the table
her speaking
singing
journey
greeting canoes with song
helps those paddling know
imparts
to children
off drugs and alcohol
talking
singing
dancing
helps those paddling know
rescues
one wooden Makah canoe

*Left by the wind*

found on Protection Island
in 1952
singing
apologizing
to it deteriorating
landlocked
at Hudson Point
the spirit of the tree
still in it
now entrusted
restored
expected to journey
helps those paddling know

Songless Dancer
preceded in death
stands on shore
awaiting the canoe
leaving behind children
and grandchildren
her speaking
singing
journey
the spirit of her tree
still in them

Her Hand

## Requiem

*For Jo Nelson*

No one to plant the marigolds
we pour libations, manure tea
brewed by thick fingers.
In the memory of her large bones
I write a text of fractured chords
the organ's open-throated baritone
edged with orange monks.
She populates my mind
from an arbor of black roses.

What is it we all regret?
Sax   sour notes
in a blues house at night?
The owl forced from his hunt
by a flap of crows?
She exacted her toll
in the bedrock of her bones
toiling furnace her body had become.
She crooned the burning fire within
her voice   a clarinet
the salt fantasy my tongue desires.

*Her pierced
body broken*

# Pink Pillbox Hat

At the hospital
Mrs. Kennedy waited
for what she already knew
her pink pillbox hat torn off
strands of hair stuck beneath the pin
She refused to change
refused another dress
shook her head
*No, let them see what they've done*

That day
the day we tumbled to despair
the rose-pink suit and pink pillbox hat
slipped from our reach –
the essence of Camelot
the essence of death

Jackie's exquisite goal
to accentuate the election
with suits taken to Dallas –
one, the pink Chanel knockoff
created in New York
for her French American taste –
pink the color of roses, azaleas,
watermelon
trimmed in navy –
blue blouse, blue pumps, blue bag
and trademark pink pillbox
secured with a pin

The first couple
the dark limousine
rounded from Houston to Elm
She wearing the hat
the world intact
then the lurch
the flash of pink panic across the trunk
her skirt wet with blood
her clothing witness
to her cradled husband's head

At the hospital
Mrs. Kennedy waited
for what she already knew

She climbed the stairs
onto Air Force One
accompanied the casket
stood beside as Lyndon took his oath
She in the suit
widowed first lady
*immaculate*
*exquisitely dressed*
*caked in blood*

The pink pillbox hopscotched
from Dallas to DC
in a heavy paper sack
from baggage handler
to White House police
to agent assigned to protect
handed from agent
to secretary

to maid
who auctioned a long list –
pink nightgown
used tube of Arden Pink lipstick
pale-blue stationery
an unopened pack
of closet-smoked Greek cigarettes
perhaps a pink pillbox hat

The widow returned
to the White House
took off the suit
and she bathed

In six months
a box arrived at the Archives –
suit, blouse, handbag, shoes,
even stockings
and an unsigned note
*Jackie's suit and bag
worn Nov. 22, 1963*

Never cleaned
unfolded
shielded from light
in an acid-free windowless room
humidity 40 percent
air changed six times an hour
precise location secret
the pink pillbox missing
the suit
brand new
except for his blood

# Artman

*For Chuck Smart*

Adrift
in dreams
Artman wanders
the soles off his shoes

Barefoot   lost
his mind
untethered
he seeks
a painful resurrection

Elegguá –
saint of open doors –
crisscross his static nightmare
lie with him
germinate his seeds
water a spectrum
of cheekbones
long legs
the arc of a foot

Elegguá –
purify him with coconut oil
throw cowry shells at his feet
beckon him
tell him –
Artman   open the door
sing the songs you like to sing
one red shoe
will show you the way

BLUES

# Letter A –
## More than a Symphony
## Chuck's Improvisation

Pancreatic duodenum
bleeds
       knots
the segregation of three
she
    I
       he
*non-percussive*
a brutal burst of timpani

*The question was about Whoopi Goldberg*
birth
octopus tendrils of black ink
his big ears syncopate

*This is the one*
an alphabet of arms
sunlight the size of the Sahara
a prick of light pierces the lens

*Can we get out of here?*
*We have to go home now*
*and water the dogs*
Nigeria's chapped lips
his bleeding palm
a cowbell alpines the air

*I remember Cedar Avenue*
grandfather's starched shirt

mother's knell in Tahoma
her siren bolero

*We're out of beef*
*Buy a boat*
a hot blade carves
skin and gut
the cat's heated yowl
sax-pursed lips

*I want upstairs*
comets cross the cold night sky
tonsils tighten
a high-pitched whine
radio echo locates
cobra's paralyzed glare

*I don't have practice being a junkie*
Feet shuffle a dark wall
antelope pictographs abandon their lair
below the flood
a pantomime of jellyfish
wash against the cutted crustacean

*God says, do you have all your stuff?*
vulva's tidal hammer
the still bloodless wood
a single peal of brine
the tip of his nail

*I have to get up now,*
*it's time to get off the bus.*

# Tiger Lament

No man remembers the time
before she called the tiger
to her breast
pink milk the taste of cherries
her hair  her rose-colored glasses
the flame in her heart not extinguished

in spring the lion and the elk rut
delinquent snow
stretches across white tundra
where polar bears roam
cubs spent on seal oil
the blubber of blue whales
fields of cracked corn
a canary yellow wing
sounds the trumpet tell
twice  thrice
the bell tolls
how can I save the tiger

the god-son bespeaks
private nuptials
wedded non-bliss
the sperm whale mates
the backyard rooster sows his seed
daffodil's bulb rooted in soil
blessed carnage
the red sacrifice of cherries
ripens in her son
his birthing awakes his libido
he sings his wild wail

a humpback song of peril
his reincarnage risen
how can I save the tiger

an acorn shell
empty of nut
barren of blood meat
she pays the rent of centuries
sun bleached
scar burnt
mischief incest wrested
her cocktail no longer fruits
her fruit no longer bleeds
her vessel no more the squeezed juice
her bit lip
pained and penniless
her blackberry teeth
shed
the shallot's powdered pepper
pewter
pomegranate
how can I save the tiger

tendrils torn from heartskin
tongue, vamp, vernal equine
ridden naked across dunes
north the swan trumpets
west the buffalo
roadbed spreads their split hooves
gravel burning
beetle's blackened carcass
a crooked cane
breaks my fall

the road batters what is left
muscle torn from bone
crippled
cusped on a blade
why do we slay the tiger

the pen's poisoned nib
flung from its shaft
weapon unwombed
hollow harrowing
wells deep
swallowed tears
I cannot keep crying
I cannot bite the wind
I cannot catch the throat shrill wail
I cannot save the chill child children
the sperm of whale
the cub
the canary's yellow wing
I cannot save the tiger
I cannot keep crying
how can I save the tiger

A painful resurrection

## Death Comes

Whose hurt cuts the deepest
the curried wound
Is mine more bitter
more burning
Is yours more stinging sweet

he is my
she was my
I am   was   will be
you are my deepest hurt

we share love's loss
a sacrament
blood cabernet and flesh biscuit
did my wine sour
did the biscuit crack your tongue
who flayed the thickest cut

winter wraps its white coat
a bear claw swipes my chest
we build a chapel of ice
fanning flame
I am his
she was my
I am forever lost without

flesh birthed
a nose has snuffled fetal hair
hormones flushed our cords
we have suckled
we entwined
I reach
your hand not there

death's contraction binds us
one womb
one heart
one breath  your breath now gone
who owns this wound of loss
whose hurt has cut the more

can I save the tiger

# Artistic Suicide

*After "Suicide Off Egg Rock," by Sylvia Plath*

It might be a year or more, she said,
till I contact you again.

Ankles stained with fatigue, she steps
into brine, brown foam, kelp's dark entangle.
A rivulet drains into the pool
where she breakfasts her feet on barnacles.

Behind her tourists in straw hats
walk the beach or lie bikini-clad
on blankets under the roar of kites,
motored biplanes on the sharp wind.
A gull tears at a greasy bag.
The stray dog yaps.

She scours the backwash
for unbroken sand dollars,
drags the sharp edge of a mussel
shell across her lip,
wrestles the moon's pull,
her tidal misgivings.

Come into me, come into me,
she hears the sea's seduction.
She does not undress.
Water rushes her lungs,
her hair a mat of kelp
and littered rose petals.
The basalt tide pushes sand into her prints.
A jellyfish floats in her hand.

# Writing Black

The black crow shuns me
sun flares stroke his wing
He caws
he highwires
he spies
I am not bread   not fruit
not road kill
He lands on my withered lawn
hops with clawed toes
He does not care my soil is parched
the blades dry
roots bound in hard pack
earthworms no longer bore
He eyes me
I am not his lover
He will not bring me tufts of down
I will die
He will pluck out my eyes
drink the blood from my lips
tear at my breast
the white of my belly will blind him
I will not hydrate the soil
I will not pool on the hardpan
He will woo the cracked crust of my body
He will fly away and feed me to his wife
He will feed me to crowlets
perched precarious
at the edge of their nest
He will leave me
a carcass for maggots to feed on
I will dry to dust   decompose
The hard pack will take me in

# The Death of Crows

Two days ago –
a crow dead at the end of my drive,
flesh and feathers pressed to pavement,
a cord of gut feathered to tar.
I shovel quills,
bones and beak,
bury them in the backyard.

Yesterday, in the same spot,
a second crow,
black beak empty and open,
his back to earth –
in dirt I bury crow next to crow.

Today a friend calls –
a third crow
dead and mangled in his yard –
Father, Son, and Holy Ghost.
He offers rum libations and incense.

It is Father's Day.
I phone my father to wish him well,
pluck I love yous from my lips.
He is deaf and cannot hear my down fall.

Crows –
your eyes, black beads, caviar my mouth,
your nailed toes open my lids,
feather quills transfuse me.
Lie still –
I will pat your wings with cinnamon oil.

Father son holy ghost

# To My Father on the Hunter's Moon

To John M. Sweet
September 29, 1924 – September 11, 2013

I.

Veteran
oil man
hunter, fisher
Alaska legislator
predictor of floods
each night
hidden behind newsprint
the armored arms of your chair

Your codes
unciphered –
food you ate from my plate
yellow stripe spray-painted on new skis
the cat you allowed
slept on your chest
gone at neighbor's complaint
silence
on my runaway ride home

I feared the night fever
of your photo on my wall
a child aching to be good
aching to be father feathered
father figure
after father
I failed

My heart became stone

A lifetime
geologic
you chiseled
coded
decoded
calculated Prudhoe Bay reserves
eyes focused
a world away
a newspaper wall away

II.

Eons eroded
your back bent
your hearing withered
you walked a deep cut
wrote
a geology of rock
and oil bled from stone

I walked
stone-anchored
canyoned from sun
cactus pricked my hide
I dipped its quill tip
words bled
slow trickle of sand from stone

Blood-mingled
I walked your deep cut
Words and photos
bonded

I printed your panoramas
near peer
in your shadow still

III.

In July
we celebrated
65 years   your wedded bliss
but to brother and I
executors
your eyes watered
your hand held your head

On 9/11
your chest pained
your heart refused to pace
your final cipher
written on the garage floor
where you were found
hours before the flood

IV.

Your bike lies on its side
your fly rod no longer flies
I edit your photos and panoramas
your chair empty
your wall fallen away

*Today*

the Earths lie down

# Toys of Childhood

*Elegy for 20 children and six adults
who died at Sandy Hook Elementary School,
Newtown, Connecticut, December 14, 2012,
with words by my father*

Blossoms of sweet peas die on the vine
under black hail, thunder
wound-pierced walls
brutal wails assault
Tear-strangled voices moan
the still-bled flesh of living and dead

Today Wall Street clamors
Today traffic jams the streets
Today nothing has changed
Today it will never be the same
Toys of childhood silenced

Yesterday Daniel was fearless
   in ripped jeans
Today Dylan no longer runs in the street
Yesterday Charlotte wore pink
Today Maddy's mom no longer waits
   at the end of the drive

Yesterday men decreed the right
   to bear arms
Today six-year-olds bleed in their seats
Yesterday there were 10
   in a Girl Scout Troop
Today five are alive
Today nothing has changed

Today it will never be the same
Toys of childhood silenced

Yesterday Josephine loved purple
Yesterday Caroline quelled fear
  in her friend
Today her friend rides alone
Yesterday Jessica loved horses and orcas
Yesterday Catherine tossed a head
  of red curls
Today Noah's twin is one

Yesterday Ben dreamed of being
  an architect
Yesterday Avielle was a spitfire
  at archery and kung fu
Yesterday Ana's family moved home
  to Newtown
where nothing had changed
where nothing will ever be the same
Toys of childhood silenced

Yesterday Chase chased balls
Yesterday James sang at the top
  of his lungs
Yesterday Jesse played with his dogs
Yesterday Jack beamed, holding his bat
Today Boy Scouts mourn their fallen
Today caskets march to their graves
Today will never be the same
Toys of childhood fallen

Yesterday Olivia led her family in grace
Yesterday Grace was a blue-eyed girl
   with gold hair
Today Emilie said *eu te amo*
   in Portuguese
Today Allison gifts kindness no more
Toys of childhood silenced

Yesterday Anne Marie taught art
Yesterday Dawn gave students all
   of her heart
Today a mother's son came unhinged
Today a mental dam broke
Today Vicki hides kids in a closet
Today Rachel, Mary, and Lauren die
   in defense

Yesterday gun shops bore gifts
   of mutton and meat
Today the lambs lie down
Today a wolf reddens the snow
Yesterday we had reason to believe
Today our prayers fall silent
Today everything has changed
Tomorrow will never be the same
Toys of childhood silenced

*I pray*

Their souls to keep

# Blessings

*On lines to be sung as a liturgical chant*

Om ~ Bless, O Lord, this food
to our use and us to thy service
and help us to be ever mindful
of the needs of others.

Now I lay me down to sleep.

Om ~ Bless, O Lord, these poems
to our mouths and us to thy service
and help us to be ever mindful
of the songs of others.

I pray the Lord my soul to keep.

Om ~ Bless, O Lord, these drums
to our hands and us to thy service
and help us to be ever mindful
of the rhythms of others.

If I should die before I wake . . .

Om ~ Bless, O Lord, this incense
to our cleansing and us to thy ember
and help us to be ever mindful
of the ritual sage.

I pray the Lord my soul to take.

Bless, O Lord, this rum to our lips
and thus to our throats

and help us to be ever mindful
of the seven-year scotch.

*In nomine Patris et Filii et Spiritus Sancti.*

Blessed be the orishas – Elegguá, Yemayá,
Obatalá, Ochún, Oggún, Ochosi, Changó,
Oduduwa, Orula, Oyá.

Bless, O Lord, this sun to our skin
and us to thy service
and help us to be ever mindful
of the heat of passion.

Blessed be Venus and Aphrodite.

Blessed be the fathers.

Blessed be the mothers.

Bless, O Lord, these chairs
to our sitting, this ground to our feet
and help us to be ever mindful
of the kneeling others.

Blessed be the Iraqis, the French,
the Germans, the British, the Irish,
the Israelis.

Now we lay us down to weep.

Blessed be the Canadians,
the Ukrainians, the Scandinavians,

the Armenians, the Palestinians.
We pray the Lord for souls he keeps.

Blessed be the Chinese,
the Balinese, the Egyptians,
the Cubans, the Puerto Ricans.

If others die in war's wake . . .

Blessed be the Rwandans,
the Ugandans, the Ashanti, the Yoruba,
the African Americans.

Pray for those our souls forsake.

Blessed be the Native Americans.

Blessed be the Mexican,
the Japanese, the Pakistani,
the white Anglo-Saxon Protestant
Americans.

Now I lay me down to sleep
I pray the Lord my soul to keep
If I should die before I wake
I pray the Lord my soul to take.

Blessed be the body, the wafer,
the blood, the wine.

Blessed be the metaphor, the abakuá,
the language of drums.

Blessed be José Martí, Dylan Thomas
and Anna Akhmatova.

Lay me down my soul to keep.

Blessed be my dog.

Blessed be the rose, petal pink lips,
full open their bloom.

Bless, O Lord, this petal to our lips
and us to thy dew mouth
and help us to be ever mindful
of the bleeding-heart sky.

Raise me up my soul to take.

Blessed be the swallow, the bat,
the gnats they pluck.

Bless, O Lord, the Stellar jay
that hops along my fence
and help me to be ever mindful
of the feeder he frequents.

Bless, O Lord, this five-bedroom house
and us to its upkeep and help us
to be ever mindful of the squirrel
in her nest built trip after trip
in long needle pine.

Now I lay me.

Help us to be ever mindful
of the carpenter ant.

My soul to keep.

Help us to be ever mindful
of the rundown tenement,
the makeshift tent in a refuge camp,
the cardboard condo under the overpass.

Om ~ Bless, O Lord, this food
to our use and us to thy service
and help us to be ever mindful
of the needs of others.

If I die . . .

I pray my soul will wake.

Help us to be ever mindful.

I pray the Lord.

Help us to be.

Help us.

Help us.

Om ~ Amen ~ Om

# House of Muscle and Bone
### *A poem within a book of poems*

Freckle face, freckleface
I am
What she once was
Mother
Mary
Washer of feet
The black
The brown
The green patine
Cherry
's first crush
A glare of rare heat
Taut muscle of calf

Mona Lisa in a black dress
The flame in her eye expires
Her life now spun
In word and song

Open
Hollow
Full of the sound of congas
She sings in drum beats
She holds back
She won't fall victim

What about the zebra?
What about the leopard?
What about the blood on your haunches?
What about the black and the white?

Ask the roots  ask the berries
Stand hours under the sun
Light a cigar
Look beneath your yellow hem

The ritual begins
Silence and slanted sunlight
Rum tears
Left by the wind   her hand
Her pierced body broken
A painful resurrection
How can I save the tiger

Father   son   holy ghost
Today the lambs lie down
I pray their souls to keep

Om ~ Amen ~ Om

# ACKNOWLDGEMENTS

Thank you to the following publications in which these works first appeared:

Breathe – *Descendant*

Cascade Anthology – *Fidel Resigns*

Conquista and Rebellion, and performed by the Miracle Theatre Group Production – *Marlin Fishing*

Examined Life: A Western Washington Poets Network Anthology – *Cello Suite*

Feminine Collective – *Listen to Your Mother*

Feminine Collective – *Mother*

Open Book: A Western Washington Poets Network Anthology – *Requiem*

Poets West Literary Journal – *Sign Language*

Pontoon #5 – *Artist's Model*

Raven Chronicles – *Mary's Song*

Seattle Erotic Art Festival Anthology – *Dis Dat*

Studio SixEight Books – *Lady Liberty: A Graphic Poem* (in the genre of graphic novels)

Studio SixEight Books – *Modeling for Chuck: A Graphic Poem* (in the genre of graphic novels)

The Black River: Death Poems – *Sign Language*

The Black River: Death Poems – *To Irene on the Anniversary of Her Death*

The Comstock Review (Poem of Special Merit) – *Songcatcher*

The Comstock Review (Poem of Special Merit) – *The Death of Crows*

*Chuck Plays Divine* – Winner, Bart Baxter Poetry in Performance Competition, 2003

*Sleep Rhythms* – Finalist, Bart Baxter Poetry in Performance Competition, 2002

*Innocents* – Finalist, Bart Baxter Poetry in Performance Competition, 2005

*Wrong Place Story* – Finalist, Bart Baxter Poetry in Performance Competition, 2007

# NOTES

Page 4. **Blood Web**. A *krathong* is a small, floating offering used in the Thai festival *Loy Krathong*.

Page 11. **Seamstress**. During "Major Snow," Mongolians kill their surplus sheep to sell or eat. A three- to four-inch incision is made with a sharp knife into the area near the heart. The aorta is then pinched with the fingers. The sheep will stop breathing immediately without much pain.

Page 15. Drawing based on a photo by Michelle Smith-Lewis.

Page 12. **Descendant**. The Hannibal Hamlin quote is from Mark Scroggins, *Hannibal: The Life of Abraham Lincoln's First Vice President* (Lanham, MD: University Press of America, 1994, 222).

Page 20. **Lady Liberty**. The inspiration for this poem was the National Park Service's shuttering of the Statue of Liberty after the 9/11 attacks in 2001.

Page 68. **Song of Chabaroka**. Chabaroka is a name that friend and collaborator Chuck Smart adopted for himself after traveling in and studying the music and instruments of Africa.

Page 85. ***Canto a los Orishas* #1**. Obatalá (Our Lady of Mercy), Elegguá (Saint Anthony), Oggún (Saint Peter), and Ochún (Our Lady of Charity) are Orishas (divine spirits), which in Cuba are associated with Catholic saints.

Page 87. ***Canto a los Orishas* #2**. Olodumare ("the owner of the source of creation that does not become empty") and Oduduwa ("the great repository which brings forth existence") are the most prominent deities in Yoruban and Cuban mythology.

Yemayá (Our Lady of Regla), Babalú-ayé (Saint Lazarus), Ochún (Our Lady of Charity, also known as Our Lady of Caridad), and Oyá (Our Lady of La

Candelaria) are Orishas associated with Catholic saints.

Page 117. **Pink Pillbox Hat**. After Faye Fiore, "Jacqueline Kennedy's Pink Pillbox Hat Is a Missing Piece of History," *The Seattle Times*, January 30, 2011.

Page 120. **Artman**. Elegguá is an Orisha associated with Saint Anthony.

Page 122. **Letter A – *More than a Symphony*, Chuck's Improvisation**. When Chuck Smart was in hospice, he asked his wife, Dawn, to write down anything that he might say, as he was in and out of consciousness. He requested that she give those words and phrases to me for a future poem. The italic lines in this poem are those phrases.

Page 124. **Tiger Lament**. After Caroline Alexander, "A Cry for the Tiger," *National Geographic*, December 2011.

Page 134. **To My Father on the Hunter's Moon**. My father, John M. Sweet, was a geologist who was involved in the discovery of oil in Alaska. After his retirement, he authored *Discovery at Prudhoe Bay: OIL!* (Hancock House Publishers, 2008).

Less than 24 hours after my father's passing on September 11, 2013, my mother and siblings had to evacuate my parents' home due to massive rains and flooding – flooding that my father had predicted.

My father also served as a legislator in the Alaska State House of Representatives. On January 3, 2014, flags across Alaska were flown at half-mast in recognition of his passing.

Page 143. **Blessings**. Obatalá (Our Lady of Mercy), Ochún (Our Lady of Charity), Oggún (Saint Peter), Ochosi (Saint Norbert), Changó (Saint Barbara), Orula (Saint Francis of Assisi), and Oyá (Our Lady of La Candelaria) are Orishas. Oduduwa is a prominent Yoruban and Cuban deity.

## ABOUT THE AUTHOR

M. Anne Sweet is a poet and artist who has performed and exhibited throughout the Pacific Northwest.

As a poet, she has performed individually, as well as with The Seattle Five Plus One, Project Z, and the Daughters of Dementia. Literary credits include a previous book-length poetry collection, *Nailed to the Sky* (Gazoobi Tales), as well as three graphic poems in the genre of graphic novels. She is a past winner of the Bart Baxter Poetry in Performance Competition, as well as having numerous works in print and online.

She maintains a working studio in the Georgetown area of Seattle, Washington, where her visual art pieces frequently combine her art and poetry. She is the recipient of several visual art and purchase awards.

Sweet has over 45 years of experience in the field of graphic design, while serving as art director, editor, and general manager for the Washington Thoroughbred Breeders and Owners Association.

She is currently learning to play upright acoustic and electric bass.